# WHAT WO...

"This is a wonderful devotional! It is filled with not only an encouraging word, but the Word, and a powerful prayer for each day. I am a firm believer in the power of our words. Joeanne has written a powerful, encouraging word for you to declare each day out of your mouth. I would suggest not just reading this once, but making it a devotional you go back to over and over again."
  **- MaryAnn Pimentel**
  Evangelist, Household of Faith Ministries

"Your faith will be lifted, your day will be better, and your relationship with Jesus will be stronger when you start your day with Joeanne Chamberlain's devotional 'Declare it!'. Word based and positive, this book is sure to help you grow in your walk with Christ."
  **- Judy Shuttlesworth**
  Author of *Raising Children with a Passion to Know and Serve Jesus Christ*

"This devotional is a great addition to your daily Bible reading. You will be strengthened as you are reminded of who you are in Christ, and it only takes a few minutes per day! It's important for a Christian to be equipped with the truth from the Word of God in order to live in victory on the earth and this book provides you with critical keys to do that. I pray you are just as blessed as I was by this devotional."
  **- Kerry Malcangi**
  Evangelist, Salvation Now

"I love this devotional! It's filled with biblical truths, prayers and declarations that lead to transformation. Highly recommend every woman to read this."
  **- Leanna Colonna**
  Author of *Relentless Faith: Port Haven Series*

# Declare it!

A 31 day devotional for women

**JOEANNE CHAMBERLAIN**

Copyright © 2023 by Joeanne Chamberlain.

All rights reserved. No portion of this book may be reproduced, stored in a retrieval system, or transmitted in any form or by any means - electronic, mechanical, photocopy, recording, scanning, or other - except for brief quotations in critical reviews or articles, without the prior written permission of the author.

The author makes no guarantees or warranties as to the accuracy, adequacy or completeness of or results to be obtained from using the content of this book and expressly disclaims any warranty expressed or implied. This limitation of liability shall apply to any claim or cause whatsoever, whether such claim or cause arises in contract, tort, or otherwise. In short, you, the reader, are responsible for your choices and the results they bring.

The scanning, uploading, and distributing of this book via the Internet or any other means without the permission of the author is illegal and punishable by law. Please purchase only authorized copies, and do not participate in or encourage piracy of copyrighted materials. Your support of the author's rights is appreciated.

Unless otherwise indicated, all Scripture quotations are taken from the Holy Bible, New Living Translation, copyright © 1996, 2004, 2015 by Tyndale House Foundation. Used by permission of Tyndale House Publishers, Inc., Carol Stream, Illinois 60188. All rights reserved.

Scripture quotations marked NIV are from THE HOLY BIBLE, NEW INTERNATIONAL VERSION®, NIV® Copyright © 1973, 1978, 1984, 2011 by Biblica, Inc.® Used by permission. All rights reserved worldwide.

Scripture quotations marked NKJV are from the New King James Version®. Copyright © 1982 by Thomas Nelson. Used by permission. All rights reserved.

First edition: June 2023

Book design by Chamberlain Creative.
Cover design by Chamberlain Creative.

ISBN: 9798397453370

www.joeannechamberlain.com

*I dedicate this book to God.*
*To God be all the glory, honour and praise.*

# PREFACE

Hi there! My name is Joeanne, and I'm so glad this book got into your hands! Whether you bought it or it was gifted to you, I pray this book is a blessing to you. I wrote this devotional with you in mind. Yes, you, the woman reading this book.

I have poured a lot of prayers into the writing of this devotional. I want this to be a blessing to every woman that reads it. This is not just a devotional to read once and put on the bookshelf. I made it 31 days long so you can read it each day of each month if you'd like to and to help these Bible truths sink into your spirit.

Speak each declaration out loud over yourself each day. Read the scripture and devotional. Pray the prayer out loud. I wrote it in first person so you can pray over yourself as you read it. Meditate on it throughout the day. I believe the Bible is the Word of God and it is truth. This devotional is based on God's Word.

If you visit my website, you can sign up to get each day's declaration on wallet-sized cards that you can print off and carry with you. You can put them on your mirror, fridge, or wherever you will see them throughout the day to remind you of these truths.

Again, I pray you would be blessed as you go through this devotional. God loves you. The best is yet to come!

# INTRODUCTION

**DECLARE**
1: to say or state (something) in an official or public way
2: to say (something) in a strong and confident way[1]

To declare something, you need to use your words. The Bible says a LOT about the importance of our words, what we speak and declare. Read the following scriptures to see just how important what we say is.

> *May the words of my mouth and the meditation of my heart be pleasing to you, O Lord, my rock and my redeemer.*
> *Psalm 19:14*
>
> *Then keep your tongue from speaking evil and your lips from telling lies!*
> *Psalm 34:13*
>
> *Take control of what I say, O Lord, and guard my lips.*
> *Psalm 141:3*
>
> *Too much talk leads to sin. Be sensible and keep your mouth shut.*
> *Proverbs 10:19*
>
> *Wise words bring many benefits, and hard work brings rewards.*
> *Proverbs 12:14*
>
> *Some people make cutting remarks, but the words of the wise bring healing.*
> *Proverbs 12:18*
>
> *A gentle answer deflects anger, but harsh words make tempers flare.*
> *Proverbs 15:1*

*Gentle words are a tree of life; a deceitful tongue crushes the spirit.*

*Proverbs 15:4*

*The heart of the godly thinks carefully before speaking, the mouth of the wicked overflows with evil words.*

*Proverbs 15:28*

*Kind words are like honey—sweet to the soul and healthy for the body.*

*Proverbs 16:24*

*A truly wise person uses few words; a person with understanding is even-tempered.*

*Proverbs 17:27*

*The tongue can bring death or life; those who love to talk will reap the consequences.*

*Proverbs 18:21*

*Watch your tongue and keep your mouth shut, and you will stay out of trouble.*

*Proverbs 21:23*

*And I tell you this, you must give an account on judgment day for every idle word you speak. The words you say will either acquit you or condemn you.*

*Matthew 12:36-37*

*It's not what goes into your mouth that defiles you; you are defiled by the words that come out of your mouth.*

*Matthew 15:11*

*But the words you speak come from the heart— that's what defiles you.*

*Matthew 15:18*

*For it is by believing in your heart that you are made right with God, and it is by openly declaring your faith that you are saved.*
*Romans 10:10*

*Don't use foul or abusive language. Let everything you say be good and helpful, so that your words will be an encouragement to those who hear them.*
*Ephesians 4:29*

*If you want to enjoy life and see many happy days, keep your tongue from speaking evil and your lips from telling lies.*
*1 Peter 3:10*

We need to take control of our words. May our words always be in line with the Word of God. When our words line up with God's Words, Satan can't touch us. As we work on changing our words, we may miss it now and then, but we can't let that get us down. We need to repent for anything wrong we've said and get right back on track. We will have what we say!

## PRAYER

Father, as I go through this devotional, I pray You will speak to me. As I begin to declare Your Words over myself, I believe I will see Your promises come to pass in my life. I want my faith to continually grow stronger and deeper in You. Help me to get my words in line with what You say. I love You Lord, and I pray this in Jesus' name. Amen.

# DAY 1

> I declare that Jesus is Lord.
> I am saved. I am a believer.

*If you openly declare that Jesus is Lord and believe in your heart that God raised him from the dead, you will be saved.*
Romans 10:9

*God saved you by his grace when you believed. And you can't take credit for this; it is a gift from God.*
Ephesians 2:8

It really is that simple. Believe in your heart that God raised Jesus from the dead and confess with your mouth that Jesus is Lord and you will be saved. God made it so easy for us to become believers. It's not because of who we are; it's because of who He is. Being saved is a gift from God. But we can't be saved if we don't openly declare it, which requires us to open our mouths and use our words.

> *But if we confess our sins to him, he is faithful and just to forgive us our sins and to cleanse us from all wickedness.*
> *1 John 1:9*

Once we are saved, we need to confess our sins and ask God for forgiveness. He is faithful to forgive us and cleanse us. When we are saved, we are a new creation.

> *This means that anyone who belongs to Christ has become a new person. The old life is gone; a new life has begun!*
> *2 Corinthians 5:17*

It's like a brand new start. We repent of our sins, God forgives us and He forgets our sins.

> *He has removed our sins as far from us as the east is from the west.*
> *Psalm 103:12*

God is so incredible!

If you are reading this and you've never given your life to God, do it now. Don't wait. It will be the best decision you ever make. All the declarations in this book are based on God's Word; for God's Word to work for you, you need to believe it as the highest truth.

SAVED: Delivered from sin and from spiritual death. Rescued from eternal punishment.[1]

If you want to give your life to God and be saved, pray this prayer.

God, I ask You to forgive me for all the sins that I have ever committed. I now thank You for forgiving me. I believe in my heart that You raised Jesus from the dead, and I confess with my mouth that Jesus is Lord! Come into my heart Lord Jesus, make me new. I choose this day to commit my life to You. In Jesus name I pray. Amen.

I remember praying a prayer similar to this when I was 23 years old. I can confidently say that accepting Jesus into my life was the best decision I have ever made. It is so beautiful to know that God wants a relationship with me. I am His daughter, and He is my God.

## PRAYER

Father, I thank You that by believing in my heart that You raised Jesus from the dead and declaring with my mouth that Jesus is Lord, I am saved. Thank You that my salvation is a gift from You. I'm so thankful You are in my life. I'm so thankful You have removed my sins from me and that You remember them no more. I thank You that Your Word is truth. Lord, I pray that You will guide me every day. As I read Your Word, I pray You will speak to me personally. I pray You will continue to work in me to make me the best version of myself that I can be. I pray this in Jesus' name. Amen.

## DAY 2

**I declare that I am a child of God.
I am a part of God's family.**

*But to all who believed him and accepted him, he gave the right to become children of God.*
*John 1:12*

*God decided in advance to adopt us into his own family by bringing us to himself through Jesus Christ. This is what he wanted to do, and it gave him great pleasure.*
*Ephesians 1:5*

How amazing is this? All we have to do is believe in Him and accept Him, and we become His children. He decided in advance that He wanted us to be a part of His family. He chose me. He chose you. Doesn't that make you want to shout? Hallelujah!

> ADOPTED: Legally made the son or daughter of someone other than a biological parent.[1]

> *"You parents—if your children ask for a loaf of bread, do you give them a stone instead? Or if they ask for a fish, do you give them a snake? Of course not! So if you sinful people know how to give good gifts to your children, how much more will your heavenly Father give good gifts to those who ask him."*
> *Matthew 7:9-11*

When we're in God's family, He is our Father. If you are a mom, you know how true this is. We would never do anything to harm our children or give them something dangerous. We only want what is best for them. When our children ask us for something, if it's good for them and we can give it to them, we do. God is a good God. If we pray to Him and ask Him for good things, things found in His Word, He will give them to us.

> *Every good gift and every perfect gift is from above, and comes down from the Father of lights, with whom there is no variation or shadow of turning.*
> *James 1:17 NKJV*

Whether you have/had a great earthly father or not, God is the ultimate and best Father there is and He is our Father when we are saved. He will never let us down.

If you didn't have a great earthly father, don't let that skew your perspective of God, our Father in Heaven. God is not a man, like an earthly father. God doesn't make mistakes as an earthly father does. God is good and only good. God loves us because we are His children. His love is unfailing, and He never stops loving us.

## PRAYER

Father, I'm so happy I am Your child! Thank You for adopting me into Your family. I thank You that You are a good God and that every good and perfect gift comes from You. I thank You, Lord, that Your Word says You give good gifts to those who ask. I know when I ask something according to Your Word, You will answer me. I pray You will speak to me as I read Your Word and that Your promises will all come to pass in my life. I pray You will give me wisdom and discernment in everything I do and say. In Jesus' name, I pray. Amen.

## DAY 3

> I declare that I am loved.
> I am loveable. I love others.

*For God so loved the world that he gave his one and only Son, that whoever believes in him shall not perish but have eternal life.*
John 3:16 NIV

*Jesus replied, "'You must love the Lord your God with all your heart, all your soul, and all your mind.' This is the first and greatest commandment. A second is equally important: 'Love your neighbor as yourself.'"*
Matthew 22:37-39

God loves us so much that He sent His son Jesus to die on the cross for us. Jesus paid our penalty so we can live forever with Him in Heaven after our lives on earth. No one will ever love us as much as God does. Not only did Jesus die on the cross for us to live in Heaven after our lives here on earth, but He also did so that we would be forgiven of all our sins and healed of all our diseases (more on that later).

God's love for us is unconditional and unlimited. God loves you, no matter who you are. You are loved! But it's up to us to accept His love. He doesn't force Himself into our lives.

> *Look! I stand at the door and knock. If you hear my voice and open the door, I will come in, and we will share a meal together as friends.*
> *Revelation 3:7*

He will knock, but it's up to us to open the door and let Him into every area of our lives and homes.

> *The Lord is not slow in keeping his promise, as some understand slowness. Instead he is patient with you, not wanting anyone to perish, but everyone to come to repentance.*
> *Peter 3:9 NIV*

God's will is that all would accept Him. God desires everyone to be saved and to experience His love. It's up to us to accept Him and His love. The sacrifice of Jesus on the cross was God's free gift to us.

WHOEVER: Whatever person, no matter who.[1]

So who is this for? Whoever believes! All we have to do is accept it. As I mentioned on Day 1, we need to believe in our hearts that God raised Jesus from the dead and confess with our mouths that Jesus is Lord (Romans 10:9).

This is how we accept God's free gift to us, by faith. Do not doubt. Just believe.

The first and greatest commandment is we need to love God. Equally as important, we need to love others.

> *Do to others as you would like them to do to you.*
>
> *Luke 6:31*

We need to treat others with respect and kindness, the way we want to be treated. When we understand the love God has for all people, including us, we will learn to love and care for our neighbours. Every soul is invaluable to God. Jesus asked His disciples, what will it profit a man if he gains the whole world, and loses his own soul? (Mark 8:36 NKJV) There is nothing on earth that has more value than a human soul.

Some people are difficult to love, but God will help us. Some people we will love from a distance, especially people that may have hurt us. We can let God heal us from the hurt, receive His love, and love others as He does.

## PRAYER

Father, I thank You for sending Your Son Jesus to die on the cross as a sacrifice for me. I thank You that You love me unconditionally. I thank You that You love me more than I can imagine. I pray You would help me to grasp how much You love me. I thank You that I am loved, and that means I am lovable. I open the door and I invite You into my life and home. Thank You for Your great love. I love You, Lord! I want to love others like You want me to, Lord. Help me to love as You love. In Jesus' name, I pray. Amen.

# DAY 4

## I declare that I am forgiven.
## I forgive others. I am free.

*He is so rich in kindness and grace that he purchased our freedom with the blood of his Son and forgave our sins.*

*Ephesians 1:7*

*Therefore if the Son makes you free, you shall be free indeed.*

*John 8:36 NKJV*

God has forgiven us of all our sins. Not only has He forgiven them, but He has also removed and forgotten them. He has removed them as far as the east is from the west (Psalm 103:12).

> SIN: An action that is considered to be wrong according to religious or moral law.[1]

If God has forgotten our sins, the wrongs we've done, once we've repented, that means He doesn't keep track of or remember them, so neither should we. Easier said than done, but we must do it.

Forgiving others isn't about letting them off the hook. It's for you! Harbouring unforgiveness will only hurt you, not them. Just as God forgives you, you need to forgive others.

> *Instead, be kind to each other, tenderhearted, forgiving one another, just as God through Christ has forgiven you.*
> *Ephesians 4:32*

> *Peter came to Jesus and asked, "Lord, how often should I forgive someone who sins against me? Seven times?" "No, not seven times," Jesus replied, "but seventy times seven!"*
> *Matthew 18:21-22*

Jesus told us to forgive and then forgive again. Forgive others with God's help, and move on.

We are now free. Free from sin, free from sickness, free from shame, free from guilt, etc. God is amazing!

> *There is now no condemnation to those who are in Christ Jesus.*
> *Romans 8:1 NKJV*

God does not condemn us. He wants us free. If you have any strongholds in your life that are not good, God can set you free from those now. Call on Him and ask Him, and He will do it.

There are many different types of strongholds one can experience. Whether it be anger issues, jealousy, pornography, drug use, etc. You will feel convicted if you have a vice in your life that isn't good for you.

If you have any strongholds in your life and you want to get rid of them, pray the following to break them off your life.

God, I know I can do all things through Christ because that is in Your Word, so I ask you to give me Your strength to break the stronghold of [*you fill in the blank*] over my life. I choose today to do my best, with Your help, to live free from all sin and evil. Amen.

Now your actions need to follow your words. Don't remain a hostage in bondage. Jesus came to set us free!

## PRAYER

Father, I thank You that I am forgiven. Lord, I forgive all who have hurt me. I thank You that I am free. I pray that if there's anything not good in my life, You will show me. I pray You will convict me and that I will know I need to make a change. When I know there's something I need to change, I pray that You will give me the strength I need to make the change. I want my actions to match my words. I pray that I will be sensitive to the Holy Spirit. I pray all this in Jesus' name. Amen.

# DAY 5

## I declare that I am chosen. God chose me.

*We know, dear brothers and sisters, that God loves you and has chosen you to be his own people.*

*1 Thessalonians 1:4*

*Even before he made the world, God loved us and chose us in Christ to be holy and without fault in his eyes.*

*Ephesians 1:4*

He chose you. He chose me. He chose us. He wanted us to be His children before we wanted Him in our lives. What a beautiful love. God has blessed us, and we are now without fault in His eyes because of what Jesus did for us.

> CHOSEN: One who is the object of choice or of divine favor.[1]

I don't know if you can relate, but I remember in elementary school, how in gym class, the teacher would pick two captains for a team sport, and then they would choose who they wanted on their team, one at a time. I was not the most athletic student, so I was often not chosen at the start, and when you're standing there, waiting to be picked, it can be disheartening. I was often picked very close to the end when there were few options left. I didn't feel like anyone wanted to choose me to be on their team; it was like they were forced to.

How wonderful is it that God has chosen us to be His! Not last, but FIRST! Even before God made the world, He loved us and chose us. So even if you feel like you're not a popular person and people don't choose you to be on their team for sports or in life, there is one, the most important One, who does choose me and you, which is a fact. We are chosen.

If you ever feel rejected by people, know that God does not reject you. Pleasing God should be our first priority. We all experience some form of rejection at some point in our lives, but that's ok. As long as we do our best to live a life pleasing to God, we know He chooses us, and that should make us smile.

> *You didn't choose me. I chose you. I appointed you to go and produce lasting fruit, so that the Father will give you whatever you ask for, using my name.*
>
> *John 15:16*

He picked us to produce lasting fruit. He says that the Father will give us whatever we ask, in Jesus' name, when we pray. It goes without saying that this is as long as it's in line with His Word. He has given us so much more than we could've thought to ask for.

## PRAYER

Father, I thank You that You love me and You chose me to be Yours. Thank You that You chose me even before You made the world. Lord, I pray You would surround me with Your love and that I would feel Your presence with me at all times. I'm glad I have chosen to accept You into my heart and have You in my life. I pray this in Jesus' name. Amen.

# DAY 6

**I declare that I can do all things through Christ who strengthens me.
God gives me strength.**

*I can do all things through Christ who strengthens me.*
                    *Philippians 4:13 NKJV*

*Don't be afraid, for I am with you. Don't be discouraged, for I am your God. I will strengthen you and help you. I will hold you up with my victorious right hand.*
                    *Isaiah 41:10*

We can do anything and everything God calls us to do.

> But don't just listen to God's word. You must do what it says. Otherwise, you are only fooling yourselves.
>
> James 1:22

Whatever God has called us to do, He will give us all we need to do it. We should not be fools. Fools will disregard the Word of God. They know what it says but don't care to obey it.

It doesn't matter if you're single or married, young or old. It doesn't matter what your background is, your economic status, where you were born or where you live. You and I can do everything God has called us to do.

STRENGTHEN: To make stronger.[1]

We are stronger than we know through Christ. God is our strength.

> The Lord is my strength and shield. I trust him with all my heart. He helps me, and my heart is filled with joy. I burst out in songs of thanksgiving.
>
> Psalm 28:7

God helps us. He fills our hearts with joy. He gives us strength.

If you are in a place where you don't feel like you can do everything you need to, take some time to pray to God and ask Him to reveal to you any changes you need to make in your life. Sometimes we take on more than we should. Sometimes we say yes to good things because we feel guilty saying no to people, but may we seek God's best and His will for our lives above trying to please others.

I've been in this place more than once. Where I've had too much on my plate and time with God gets pushed aside. I've had to go to God, repent, and ask Him to help me go through my schedule and see where I need to make changes. He has helped me to get back on track with where I should be. I know He will help you, too, if you want Him to.

We need to ask God to guide us so we only do and take on what God wants us to. We need to learn to say no, even to good things sometimes. God wants the best for us. If we want His best, we need to be sensitive to the Holy Spirit guiding us. We need to make sure we are making time for God each day, first and foremost.

God tells us not to fear. God tells us not to be discouraged. He will strengthen us and help us. God will hold us up. Let us have confidence in God to do what He says He will do.

## PRAYER

Father, I thank You that I can do all things through Christ who strengthens me. I thank You that I am able to do everything You have called me to do because You have given me all I need to do it. I pray You would reveal anything I may have started doing or I'm currently doing that is not something You want me to do. I only want to do what You've called me to do. When opportunities present themselves, and invitations come, give me discernment in when to say yes and when to say no. Thank You that You are with me, so I do not need to be afraid or discouraged. Thank You that You strengthen me and help me and hold me up. In Jesus' name, I pray. Amen.

## DAY 7

### I declare that I am healed.
### I am healthy. I will live a long life.

*Surely he took up our pain and bore our suffering, yet we considered him punished by God, stricken by him, and afflicted. But he was pierced for our transgressions, he was crushed for our iniquities; the punishment that brought us peace was on him, and by his wounds we are healed.*
Isaiah 53:4-5 NIV

*My child, pay attention to what I say. Listen carefully to my words. Don't lose sight of them. Let them penetrate deep into your heart, for they bring life to those who find them, and healing to their whole body.*
Proverbs 4:20-22

*I will reward them with a long life and give them my salvation.*
Psalm 91:16

Jesus not only died on the cross to forgive us of all our sins; He was wounded so we can be healed. How amazing is our God? Jesus Christ is the same yesterday, today and forever (Hebrews 13:8), and Jesus healed all when He was on this earth that reached out to Him for it. He took care of everything concerning us; our spirit, our soul and our physical body.

> HEAL: To make free from injury or disease, to make sound or whole. To make well again, to restore to health.[1]

Jesus was wounded before He went to the cross so that we could be healed. It's already done. It's already paid for.

> *Let all that I am praise the Lord; may I never forget the good things he does for me. He forgives all my sins and heals all my diseases.*
> *Psalm 103:2-3*

If anything is affecting your body from operating and functioning as it should, pray to God right now and ask Him to heal you and thank Him that it is done. Have faith rise up in your heart right now to believe it and take it.

Healing may happen instantly, or it may be gradual, but stay in faith, and the healing will manifest. Don't let negative words come out of your mouth. Stand on God's promises. Trust His Word. Keep declaring, "By Jesus' stripes, I was healed, so I am healed. Healing is mine now."

As we let God's Word fill our hearts and minds, they give us life and keep us healthy! God's Word does not return to Him void, but it accomplishes that for which it was sent (Isaiah 55:11). God keeps His promises!

> *My child, listen to me and do as I say, and you will have a long, good life. I will teach you wisdom's ways and lead you in straight paths.*
> *Proverbs 4:10-11*

God also tells us that He rewards us with long life. This is a wonderful promise to grab hold of, knowing God keeps His Word.

If you'd like to know more on this topic of healing, I highly recommend reading the book *Healing The Sick* by TL Osborn. I have a list of some of my favourite books at the back of this book, and this one is on that list.

## PRAYER

Father, I thank You that You sent Your Son Jesus to die on the cross and all that was accomplished through that. I thank You that You not only forgive all my sins, but You heal all diseases. Lord, I pray that healing will manifest in my body now. I pray anything that is not of You leaves my body now. I ask You to heal me from the top of my head to the soles of my feet, from the inside out. Restore me to perfect health and make me whole. I thank You that it is Your will for me to be healed and walk in health. I also thank You that Your Word says You will satisfy me with a long life. I thank You for keeping Your promises. I thank You for my healing, and I give You all the glory. I pray this in Jesus' name. Amen.

# DAY 8

**I declare that I am joyful.
I rejoice in the Lord always.
I am filled with joy.**

*Always be full of joy in the Lord. I say it again—rejoice!*
*Philippians 4:4*

*I have told you these things so that you will be filled with my joy. Yes, your joy will overflow!*
*John 15:11*

Joy is not the same as happiness, and though it is wonderful to be happy, we should aim to be joyful always. God wants us to have joy.

> ... the joy of the Lord is your strength!
> Nehemiah 8:10

To be strong, we need the joy of the Lord. When we read the Word of God, we are filled with joy.

> For all of God's promises have been fulfilled in Christ with a resounding "Yes!" And through Christ, our "Amen" (which means "Yes") ascends to God for his glory.
> 2 Corinthians 1:20

We can't help but be joyful when we know God's Word and the promises in it. When we are filled with this joy, it will overflow.

OVERFLOW: To flow over the brim of.[1]

The way I see it, if we are told that our joy will overflow, it will be seen. It's not something we keep hidden inside. Others will see us with this joy. Have you ever noticed that when you smile at someone, even a stranger, most of the time, they smile back? I've done this. I often smile at people as I walk past them, and most of the time, they smile back. Try it sometime. It's almost as though joy is contagious.

Knowing what we know about our God, who we are because of Him, and all His promises, we should be full of joy. I think of the Sunday School song,

> "I have the joy, joy, joy, joy,
> Down in my heart, (where?)
> Down in my heart, (where?)
> Down in my heart,
> I have the joy, joy, joy, joy,
> Down in my heart, (where?)
> Down in my heart to stay.

> And I'm so happy, so very happy
> I have the love of Jesus in my heart.
> (Down in my heart)
> And I'm so happy, so very happy
> I have the love of Jesus in my heart."[2]

Joy is the love of Jesus in our hearts. We know God loves us, so we have the love of Jesus in our hearts; therefore, let us be full of joy.

> *I pray that God, the source of hope, will fill you completely with joy and peace because you trust in him. Then you will overflow with confident hope through the power of the Holy Spirit.*
> Romans 15:13

God will fill us completely with joy and peace as we trust in Him. Do you want to be filled with joy and peace? I know I do. Let us trust in Him.

## PRAYER

Father, I thank You that the joy of the Lord is my strength. I will rejoice in You every day, Lord. I will give thanks to You every day. I will not allow the circumstances around me to steal the joy that You have given me. I know Your promises are all yes and amen, so I will rejoice in You. I trust in You. Please fill me completely with joy and peace. I want to be filled with joy that overflows! I pray this in Jesus' name. Amen.

# DAY 9

## I declare that I am sheltered by God. I am shielded. I am protected.

*Those who live in the shelter of the Most High will find rest in the shadow of the Almighty.*
*Psalm 91:1*

*He will cover you with his feathers, and under his wings you will find refuge; his faithfulness will be your shield and rampart.*
*Psalm 91:4 NIV*

*The Lord says, "I will rescue those who love me. I will protect those who trust in my name.*
*Psalm 91:14*

Have you ever seen how a mother hen covers her chicks with her wings to keep them safe from evil predators? God keeps us under His wings in safety.

Do you love God? You should. When you love God, He will rescue you. Do you trust in God's name? You should. When you trust in His name, He will protect you. A shelter covers and protects. God is our shelter, He alone keeps us safe. We don't need to worry or have fear.

> *The godly will rejoice in the Lord and find shelter in him. And those who do what is right will praise him.*
> *Psalm 64:10*

PROTECT: To cover or shield from exposure, injury, damage, or destruction.[1]

As a mother, I want to protect my son from all bad and evil, and if that's my heart for my son, I know that God wants that for him, me, and you, too, because we are His children.

God will keep us shielded from exposure, injury, damage and destruction. In our world, it's so comforting to know that we have a God that will keep us safe from all harm and evil.

> *The Lord is my rock, my fortress, and my savior; my God is my rock, in whom I find protection. He is my shield, the power that saves me, and my place of safety.*
> *Psalm 18:2*

How do we live in the shelter of the Most High? We read the Bible and do what God instructs us to do. Stay away from sin. These promises don't just work automatically. We have our part to play. When we do our part, God is always faithful to do His.

If you slip and make a mistake, don't wait to make it right. Repent. Ask God to forgive you and get right back on track so you can get back under the shelter of the almighty, where you can be safe and free from danger.

Psalm 91 is my favourite Psalm. It's one of my favourite passages in the entire Bible. It has many incredible protection promises that we can stand on and trust God will do His part when we love and obey Him.

## PRAYER

Father, I thank You that You cover me like a mother hen covers her chicks. I thank You that as I obey Your Word, I live in Your shelter and can find rest in You. I thank You that You will cover me with Your feathers, and under Your wings, I will find refuge. I am so thankful for Your protection. Because I love You, God, and because I trust in Your name, I know that You will rescue me and protect me. I pray this in Jesus' name. Amen.

## DAY 10

### I declare that I am held securely. I am safe. I sleep well at night.

*We know that God's children do not make a practice of sinning, for God's Son holds them securely, and the evil one cannot touch them.*
                                    1 John 5:18

*In peace I will lie down and sleep, for you alone, O Lord, will keep me safe.*
                                    Psalm 4:8

*You can go to bed without fear; you will lie down and sleep soundly.*
                                    Proverbs 3:24

If we do our part, obey God and don't sin, God will keep us so secure that the evil one cannot touch us. That is awesome protection to have! We must do our part, stay away from evil and do as God's Word instructs us to stay safe and secure.

SECURE: Free from danger.[1]

God wants to keep us protected. He also wants to keep us secure. God doesn't want anything bad to happen to us. He is a good God. He is not the author of evil or danger. He wants to keep things from the enemy far from us, and He will when we obey Him and stay close to Him.

When we go to sleep at night, we can sleep well.

*...for he grants sleep to those he loves.*
*Psalm 127:2 NIV*

God keeps us safe and protected during the day and at night, even when we sleep. 24/7 protection.

*He will not let you stumble; the one who watches over you will not slumber.*
*Psalm 121:3*

God is always watching over us. God doesn't sleep.

*Those who fear the Lord are secure; he will be a refuge for their children.*
*Proverbs 14:26*

Not only does God keep us secure when we fear Him, but He will be a refuge for our children. That definitely gives me peace as a mother. Since I know that I'm not with my son 24/7, even when I'm not beside him, I know God is keeping him secure.

*The name of the Lord is a strong fortress; the godly run to him and are safe.*
*Proverbs 18:10*

If we run to God, we are safe. He is our refuge.

When my son was an infant and would wake up every 2 hours, and did so for six months straight, the lack of sleep at that time greatly affected my body. However, it was out of my control. But I've had times when I was not sleeping well due to nightmares and too many things on my mind, and it started to affect my body, not in a good way. So I began to meditate on God's Word before bed, reciting these scriptures about sleep, and I found that it helped a lot.

If you've ever gone through a season where you were not sleeping well, you know it does affect you. A lack of sleep can make you tired, weak, lethargic, cause anxiety, etc. Rest assured, it is God's will for us, His children, to sleep well at night. Read these scriptures before bed. Meditate on them if you are not sleeping well. Rest in God, knowing He will take care of you.

## PRAYER

Father, I pray You would equip me with all that I need to ensure that I do not sin, so I can know that I'm held securely by You and that the evil one cannot touch me. I do not have to fear because You are watching over me 24 hours a day, seven days a week. I thank You that You give sweet sleep to those You love, and I thank You that You love me. I can go to bed without fear, and I will sleep soundly. I pray I would sleep well every night, and every day I would wake up feeling refreshed and energized. I pray this in Jesus' name. Amen.

## DAY 11

I declare that I study and meditate on God's Word.
I live according to God's Word.
I am a student of the Word.

*Study this Book of Instruction continually. Meditate on it day and night so you will be sure to obey everything written in it. Only then will you prosper and succeed in all you do.*
*Joshua 1:8*

*All Scripture is inspired by God and is useful to teach us what is true and to make us realize what is wrong in our lives. It corrects us when we are wrong and teaches us to do what is right. God uses it to prepare and equip his people to do every good work.*
*2 Timothy 3:16-17*

This is so important. We need to get the Word in us, not by reading it once and putting it back on a bookshelf, but by reading it daily. The Bible gives us instruction, helps us prosper, brings healing to our whole body, keeps us under God's protection, and guides us in the way we should go. We need the Word to come alive in us so that no matter what is thrown our way, we have God's Word in us as the answer.

We can succeed in all we do, but only by keeping God first. When we read scripture, it will convict us with changes we need to make in our lives. The Word will come alive in us as we keep reading and obeying it. This is how we stay safe and protected by God.

MEDITATE: To engage in contemplation or reflection.[1]

We need to meditate and reflect on God's Word as we read it. We sould think about God's Word as we go about our day. The more of God's Word in us, the better equipped we will be as His children to do every good work.

When Jesus was in the desert, and Satan tempted him, Jesus used the Word of God to fight back.

> *But Jesus told him, "No! The Scriptures say, 'People do not live by bread alone.'"*
> *Luke 4:4*
>
> *Jesus replied, "The Scriptures say, 'You must worship the Lord your God and serve only him.'"*
> *Luke 4:8*
>
> *Jesus responded, "The Scriptures also say, 'You must not test the Lord your God.'"*
> *Luke 4:12*

The Word of God is a weapon. We can only use the Word of God as a weapon against the enemy if we know the Word. We need to study God's Word. We can read through the Bible each year, a passage of the Bible each day. We can study different topics and subjects in it too. The more we study and learn, the more we will know and the better it is for us.

Just like Jesus spoke back to the devil out loud with the Word of God, we can do the same. When the devil comes and whispers lies to us or tells us things that we know are not in God's Word or we know are the opposite of God's will, we can use the Word of God and send the devil back to where he belongs.

> *So humble yourselves before God. Resist the devil, and he will flee from you.*
>
> James 4:7

## PRAYER

Father, I thank You that I have a Bible to read, which is Your Word. I thank You that as I study Your Word and meditate on it, I will live according to Your Word. I want to be a good student. I thank You that the more I read Your Word, the more it will fill me so that I can be prepared no matter what comes my way. I pray that You would speak to me through Your Word. I pray You would help me to retain Your Word in my heart and that Your Words would always be on my lips. Thank You that as I humble myself before You, I can speak to the devil using Your Words, and he has to flee. In Jesus' name, I pray. Amen.

## DAY 12

> I declare that I am wearing
> the armour of God.
> I put on the whole armour of God.

*A final word: Be strong in the Lord and in his mighty power. Put on all of God's armor so that you will be able to stand firm against all strategies of the devil. For we are not fighting against flesh-and-blood enemies, but against evil rulers and authorities of the unseen world, against mighty powers in this dark world, and against evil spirits in the heavenly places. Therefore, put on every piece of God's armor so you will be able to resist the enemy in the time of evil. Then after the battle you will still be standing firm. Stand your ground, putting on the belt of truth and the body armor of God's righteousness. For shoes, put on the peace that comes from the Good News so that you will be fully prepared. In addition to all of these, hold up the shield of faith to stop the fiery arrows of the devil. Put on salvation as your helmet, and take the sword of the Spirit, which is the word of God.*

Ephesians 6:10-17

The devil is our greatest adversary, and it's so great to know Jesus Christ has already defeated him. But we don't fight him as humans fight; we fight him in the spiritual realm.

> *We are human, but we don't wage war as humans do. We use God's mighty weapons, not worldly weapons, to knock down the strongholds of human reasoning and to destroy false arguments. We destroy every proud obstacle that keeps people from knowing God. We capture their rebellious thoughts and teach them to obey Christ...*
> 
> *2 Corinthians 10:3-5*

God has given us armour that if we wear it, we will never be defeated. In the NKJV translation, verse 16 reads: above all, taking the shield of faith with which you will be able to quench all the fiery darts of the wicked one. Satan cannot win. We have victory every time because of Jesus. We must stay in the Word and keep holding up the shield of faith at all times.

> *The Lord will conquer your enemies when they attack you. They will attack you from one direction, but they will scatter from you in seven!*
> 
> *Deuteronomy 28:7*

ARMOR: Defensive covering for the body.[1]

It's not difficult to put on all this armour. It's easier than you think. But it's also a choice. We need to choose to put on this armour. If we will read God's Word daily, believe what it says, obey it and live according to it, we are putting on the armour of God. God doesn't leave any part of us uncovered. A lot of people say what about our backs?

*...for the Lord will go before you, the God of Israel will be your rear guard.*
Isaiah 52:12 NIV

God is our rear guard, so He's got our backs. Talk about being fully covered by God. When we do our part, God always does His part. I'm so thankful God has given us the tools to stand strong. God not only keeps us safe and protected 24/7, but He also protects us from every direction.

## PRAYER

Father, thank You that You are good, and You have given me everything I need in Your Word. Thank You for the armour that You've provided for me. That when I read Your Word, listen to it, believe it as true, obey it and live by it, I am putting on the full armour. I thank You that I have a shield of faith that I can hold up, and it quenches all the enemy's fiery darts. I pray that You would help me do my part and put on the full armour, so that You can do your part and keep me protected at all times. In Jesus' name, I pray. Amen.

## DAY 13

### I declare that I am wise. I have wisdom.

*If you need wisdom, ask our generous God, and he will give it to you. He will not rebuke you for asking.*

*James 1:5*

I love that God wants us to ask for wisdom, and He will give it to us. He doesn't ask us why we want it; He doesn't tell us we should already have it. He won't rebuke us for asking. So let us ask every day for wisdom so we make the right choices and decisions and stay in His good, pleasing and perfect will for our lives (Romans 12:2).

We gain lots of wisdom through reading the Bible. We can also gain wisdom through reading books and listening to podcasts of men and women of God. God will speak to us however He wants to, we can't limit Him. He will give us wisdom, all we have to do is ask.

> WISDOM: The natural ability to understand things that most other people cannot understand. Good sense or judgement.[1]

Wisdom provides us with the ability to understand things most people cannot. It gives us the ability to discern what is important. We need to know right from wrong. We need to know the truth from lies. We never get to a point where we know it all and don't need God to give us wisdom.

> *For the Lord grants wisdom! From his mouth come knowledge and understanding.*
> *Proverbs 2:6*

If we ask God for wisdom, He will give it to us for big decisions like where to go to school, what house to buy, who to marry, and smaller decisions like which route to take to work, which movies we should or shouldn't watch, and what music we should or shouldn't listen to, etc.

> *But the wisdom from above is first of all pure. It is also peace loving, gentle at all times, and willing to yield to others. It is full of mercy and the fruit of good deeds. It shows no favoritism and is always sincere.*
> *James 3:17*

This is the wisdom God will give us if we ask for it.

We need to get in God's Word; it is full of wisdom. Proverbs is a book with lots of wisdom in it.

> *Fear of the Lord is the foundation of true knowledge, but fools despise wisdom and discipline.*
>
> *Proverbs 1:7*

Don't be a fool. You're better than that. If God's Word doesn't have a clear answer for the wisdom you are seek (like where to live, who to marry, etc) pray and ask God, and He will give you the wisdom and discernment to make the right decision. The book of Proverbs is so full of wisdom. I read through it a few times a year, and I suggest you do too.

## PRAYER

Father, I thank You for being a gracious God. You hear my prayers and answer them. Lord, I don't want to be a fool. I want to be wise. As I read Your Word, I pray that You will give me wisdom. I want Your good, perfect and pleasing will for my life. When there are decisions that I need to make that aren't clear in Your Word, I pray that You will give me the wisdom and discernment to make the right choices. Teach me right from wrong, teach me to know the truth from lies. I pray this in Jesus' name. Amen.

## DAY 14

**I declare that I am a conqueror.
I overcome evil with good.
I have authority over the enemy.**

*Don't let evil conquer you, but conquer evil by doing good.*

*Romans 12:21*

*Look, I have given you authority over all the power of the enemy, and you can walk among snakes and scorpions and crush them. Nothing will injure you.*

*Luke 10:19*

Praise the Lord! Nothing will injure us. God has a shield of protection around us. The devil cannot hurt us. He will try, but we can stand on God's Word, and no harm can come to us when we do. Let us keep God first in our hearts and lives, and we will be conquerors. We need to keep the whole armour of God on us at all times.

> AUTHORITY: The power to give orders or make decisions. The power or right to direct or control someone or something.[1]

The enemy will attack, it's what he does, but we have the armour of God and the authority God has given us to combat his attacks. Martin Luther said, "You cannot keep birds from flying over your head, but you can keep them from building a nest in your hair." That is so true. The enemy will attack, and he will send us thoughts that are not good, but we can choose not to dwell on those thoughts and instead dwell on God's promises in His Word.

> *The thief does not come except to steal, and to kill, and to destroy. I have come that they may have life, and that they may have it more abundantly.*
> *John 10:10 NKJV*

If it steals, kills or destroys, it is not from God; it's from the enemy. We have the authority to speak to the devil and send him back to where he belongs. We can do this by using the authority we have and the power in the name of Jesus.

> *When the seventy-two disciples returned, they joyfully reported to him, "Lord, even the demons obey us when we use your name!"*
> *Luke 10:17*

The disciples said demons were subject to them in Jesus' name. We are Jesus' disciples, and we have that same authority in us.

This sounds too good to be true, but God is just that good. So when the enemy attacks, remember who you are, a child of God with armour on and authority over the enemy. Tell the devil to back off. He will attack, but no weapon will prosper against a child of God.

## PRAYER

Father, thank You so much for giving me authority over the enemy. He is under my feet! When the enemy attacks, I will stand firm in my faith and use the authority You have given to me to send the devil back to where he came from. I pray You will help me overcome evil with good all the time. I thank You that Your Word says nothing will injure me. Keep me safe and empower me to use the authority You've given me. I love You, Lord. I pray this in Jesus' name. Amen.

# DAY 15

> I declare that I am victorious.
> I live in victory.
> I use God's mighty weapons.

*But you belong to God, my dear children. You have already won a victory over those people, because the Spirit who lives in you is greater than the spirit who lives in the world.*
*1 John 4:4*

*We use God's mighty weapons, not worldly weapons, to knock down the strongholds of human reasoning and to destroy false arguments. We destroy every proud obstacle that keeps people from knowing God. We capture their rebellious thoughts and teach them to obey Christ.*
*2 Corinthians 10:4-5*

We have already won the victory over the evil one because the Holy Spirit in us is greater than the devil. So we tear down the lies of the enemy (false arguments) that would contradict God's Word, and we make our thoughts align with what God says.

This goes hand in hand with yesterday's reading. We have authority over the enemy. One of the places he likes to mess with us most is in our thoughts. But we can capture those thoughts and make them obedient to God's Word. It takes practice, but if we practice this, it will help us out immensely.

> *But thank God! He gives us victory over sin and death through our Lord Jesus Christ.*
> *1 Corinthians 15:57*

VICTORY: Success in defeating an opponent or enemy.[1]

We have the Spirit of God in us; because of that, we have victory every time over the enemy because God's Spirit in us is greater than the enemy. When Jesus died on the cross and then rose from the dead, He defeated Satan once and for all.

It's up to us to choose to live in the victory that was won for us. We have to do our part. We need to take every thought captive. We need to teach our thoughts to obey Christ. When we think something that doesn't line up with God's Word, we can make sure to change our thinking, and that's where meditating on God's Word comes into play. Victory begins in our minds.

> *And now, dear brothers and sisters, one final thing. Fix your thoughts on what is true, and honorable, and right, and pure, and lovely, and admirable. Think about things that are excellent and worthy of praise.*
> *Philippians 4:8*

We need to think about these things. I, for one, don't listen to the news. I'd rather not fill myself with that information because the news is not very positive or uplifting. It's quite the opposite. I want to think 'God thoughts'. I want victory in every area of life, and I'm sure you do too.

> *For every child of God defeats this evil world, and we achieve this victory through our faith. And who can win this battle against the world? Only those who believe that Jesus is the Son of God.*
> 
> 1 John 5:4-5

We achieve this victory through our faith. Faith comes by hearing the Word of God, reading the Bible and meditating on God's Words. Victory belongs to us as God's children. Let us grab hold of our victory and stand firm in our faith.

## PRAYER

Father, I thank You that Your Spirit lives in me and that because of this, I always have victory over the enemy. Thank You that because Jesus defeated Satan, Satan now has no power over me! Help me recognize when thoughts don't line up with Your Word, and take every thought captive that doesn't line up, and make it obedient to Your Word. Thank You for the victory. I pray this in Jesus' name. Amen.

## DAY 16

**I declare that I have a sound mind. I will not fear. I have the mind of Christ.**

*For God has not given us a spirit of fear, but of power and of love and of a sound mind.*
2 Timothy 1:7 NKJV

*For, "Who can know the Lord's thoughts? Who knows enough to teach him?" But we understand these things, for we have the mind of Christ.*
1 Corinthians 2:16

FEAR: An unpleasant often strong emotion caused by anticipation or awareness of danger.[1]

We have learned that God keeps us protected and watches over us 24/7. In Psalm 121, we read that God doesn't sleep or slumber. So if we know we are safe and protected because we are obeying God, we have no reason to fear. We know God protects us from danger.

Don't get me wrong; I am not saying that I've never been afraid; I have been. But when fear comes knocking, we must find out why and answer with faith in God's Word and who He is.

Fear is not from God. God doesn't want us to fear. So we need to cast out the spirit of fear. God has given us the Holy Spirit. He also gives us a Spirit of power, love and a sound mind. We don't need to let our minds wander and let the enemy mess with us in our thoughts. We can choose what we think about. God has given us the mind of Christ. We need to get in His Word and meditate on it. Meditating on God's Word will help us keep our minds focused on truth.

We cannot let the devil mess with our thoughts. The mind is a battlefield. Our thoughts are where the enemy tries to attack. Our thoughts are real to us, so we need to think about what we're thinking about. We should not be expecting danger. We should expect God to keep His Word and for good things to happen to us.

We need to make sure we don't think about the negative thoughts the enemy throws at us and dwell in fear, but we need to think God thoughts. Then we will have victory and a sound mind.

I cannot stress enough how important it is to get in God's Word. Study it. Find promises in it. Read books about it. Listen to songs about it. Listen to people preach on it.

*For the word of God is alive and active...*
*Hebrews 4:12 NIV*

*For the word of the Lord is right and true; he is faithful in all he does.*

*Psalm 33:4 NIV*

It's in His Word that we find all we need. God's Word is alive, active, right and true. It guides us and directs us in the ways we should go. God is faithful. Reject fear and thank God for a sound mind.

## PRAYER

Father, thank You that You have not given me a spirit of fear, but You've given me a Spirit of power, love and a sound mind. Thank You that I do not have to be afraid of anything. Thank You that I can have the mind of Christ. Lord, help me do my part and get so into Your Word that this is my truth. If there's any fear right now in my life, I command it to get lost. I don't want it. I stand on Your Word and truth. I pray this in Jesus' name. Amen.

# DAY 17

## I declare that I am rooted in Christ.

*Let your roots grow down into him, and let your lives be built on him. Then your faith will grow strong in the truth you were taught, and you will overflow with thankfulness.*
*Colossians 2:7*

We need to be rooted in Christ. To do this, we need to plant the seed (The Word) and water the seed. We water it by continuing to read the Word and learning more. As our roots grow deeper, we grow stronger in our faith, and nothing can shake us. We will overflow with thankfulness because we will know who we are in Christ.

We need to press in and go deeper into the Word. Using a study Bible can be helpful. Search out men and women of God that are preaching the full Gospel and listen to their teachings. What do I mean when I say the full Gospel? I mean not just teaching forgiveness of sins, but also teaching divine healing, the baptism of the Holy Spirit, and everything in the Bible. Put into practice what you learn.

You may or may not know the parable of the farmer scattering seed. If not, check it out in Mark Chapter 4. I want to bring attention to two parts.

> *The seed on the rocky soil represents those who hear the message and immediately receive it with joy. But since they don't have deep roots, they don't last long. They fall away as soon as they have problems or are persecuted for believing God's word.*
> 
> *Mark 4:16-17*

They didn't have deep roots, so they fell away quickly when problems came.

> *And the seed that fell on good soil represents those who hear and accept God's word and produce a harvest of thirty, sixty, or even a hundred times as much as had been planted!*
> 
> *Mark 4:20*

If you have good soil, which is the condition of your heart, your roots will grow strong, deep, and immovable, and you will produce a harvest.

ROOT: The part of a plant that grows underground, gets water from the ground, and holds the plant in place.[1]

The roots are the part of the plant that grows underground. Roots are usually not seen. What are you doing when no one else is watching? If you go to church Sunday morning, that's great. But are you reading the Bible, praying, and learning more about God from Monday to Saturday?

The roots get water from the ground; that's how the roots "eat" to help them grow. The quiet time in the Word and prayer is where you get filled up so your roots grow in Him. As we do this, our faith will grow stronger, and we will be immovable as a strong tree whose roots are so far into the ground that we cannot be uprooted.

## PRAYER

Father, I hunger and thirst for You, to know You better. As I read Your Word daily, I pray You would speak to me, that it would sink into my spirit and be absorbed so that my roots keep growing in You and my faith grows stronger each day. I do not want to be movable. I want to stand firm in my faith and not waver. Thank You for wanting me to be strong in the truth I am taught. Please guide me to the right teachings to listen to each week to help build my faith. In Jesus' name, I pray. Amen.

## DAY 18

> I declare that I am strong
> and courageous.
> I will stand firm in faith.

*This is my command- be strong and courageous! Do not be afraid or discouraged. For the Lord your God is with you wherever you go."*
*Joshua 1:9*

*Be on guard. Stand firm in the faith. Be courageous. Be strong.*
*1 Corinthians 16:13*

God tells us to not be afraid or discouraged. How often do we feel that way? More than we should. But we need to do what God tells us to do. We need to be strong and courageous because God is always with us wherever we go.

I don't believe God is talking about being physically strong here. I believe that if we need physical strength to accomplish what He is asking us to do, He will give it to us. But I think here He is talking about being strong in Spirit - a strength in knowing that God is always with us.

God will guide us when we pray and use wisdom in our decisions. We can't live in sin deliberately and expect God to be with us. But as long as we do our best with what we know, He will always be with us.

> *Be strong and courageous. Do not be afraid or terrified because of them, for the Lord your God goes with you; he will never leave you nor forsake you.*
> *Deuteronomy 31:6 NIV*

We need to stand firm in our faith. We can be strong because God is with us.

> *Let us hold tightly without wavering to the hope we affirm, for God can be trusted to keep his promise.*
> *Hebrews 10:23*

FIRM: Securely or solidly fixed in place.[1]

Stand firm. God's got us. We can do everything He has called us to do and go everywhere He calls us to go without fear.

Like we read yesterday, if we let our roots grow deep, we become immovable in God's Word, and that's how we stand firm.

*So be strong and courageous, all you who put your hope in the Lord!*

*Psalm 31:24*

*But those who trust in the Lord will find new strength. They will soar high on wings like eagles. They will run and not grow weary. They will walk and not faint.*

*Isaiah 40:31*

God will strength us when we put our hope and trust in Him. We won't grow weary. We are strong and stronger than we know with God in us!

## PRAYER

Father, I thank You that as I do my best to obey You, I know and can rest assured that You are always with me; You never leave me or forsake me. I can be strong and courageous and do all You have asked me to do and go everywhere You tell me to go. I do not have to be afraid or discouraged. I pray that You help me stand firm in faith without wavering, so I can always be strong and courageous. In Jesus' name, I pray. Amen.

# DAY 19

> I declare that I am prosperous.
> I am rich. I am provided for.
> God gives me everything I need.

*They are like trees planted along the riverbank, bearing fruit each season. Their leaves never wither, and they prosper in all they do.*
*Psalm 1:3*

*You know the generous grace of our Lord Jesus Christ. Though he was rich, yet for your sakes he became poor, so that by his poverty he could make you rich.*
*2 Corinthians 8:9*

*Seek the Kingdom of God above all else, and live righteously, and he will give you everything you need.*
*Matthew 6:33*

God wants us to prosper in every way, and that includes financially. His Word tells us to test Him in the area of finances, that if we tithe and give offerings, He will pour out blessings so great we won't have room enough to contain them. (Malachi 3:10) God knows our hearts. He knows if we want to give to God's Kingdom and keep doing so, the more we make, the more we'll give back to Him. If we keep doing this, God will continue to bless us.

People don't like to talk much about money and tithing. Yet, it is a big topic in the Bible, and if you don't know much about it, doing a study would be beneficial. God wants to bless us so we can be a blessing. He doesn't only give us what we need because we wouldn't be able to bless others if that were the case.

If you don't know, a tithe is 10%. According to the Bible, we should be tithing 10% on all that comes to us.

> RICH: Having abundant possessions and especially material wealth.[1]

Becoming rich doesn't necessarily happen overnight. But as we do our part with what we have and are faithful in tithing and offerings, we need to trust that God's Word is true. Be wise. If you don't think you are "rich" right now, you may need to make some changes. Live within your current means. If you must choose between tithing or saving for a family vacation, tithe! And trust God that He will provide for that family vacation. Don't spend your money foolishly. Sow seeds, believing that you will reap a harvest.

> *Remember this: Whoever sows sparingly will also reap sparingly, and whoever sows generously will also reap generously. Each of you should give what you have decided in your heart to give, not reluctantly or under compulsion, for God loves a cheerful giver.*
> *2 Corinthians 9:6-7 NIV*

The more you sow, the more you reap. God wants us to give cheerfully. Give with a smile on your face, knowing that God will do what He says He will do in His Word. But you must be tithing, giving offerings and obeying the Lord's instructions.

Also, change your language. Don't say, "I can't afford that!" or "I could never spend that much." Instead, say, "I'll be back for that later". God wants us to prosper in all we do, in every season. If we are not, let us pray and ask God to give us wisdom and direction to help us get to the point where we are not only blessed but also a blessing.

> *But remember the Lord your God, for it is he who gives you the ability to produce wealth, and so confirms his covenant, which he swore to your ancestors, as it is today.*
> *Deuteronomy 8:18 NIV*

God gives us the ability to produce wealth, so let us ask Him for a God idea!

## PRAYER

Father, I thank You that Jesus became poor so I could be rich. Even if I don't see it in the natural right now, I am trusting that as I am faithful in tithing 10% of everything I make, as I give offerings and sow seeds, I know that You will bless me more than I can imagine so I can give more and be a blessing to others. Your Word tells me You give me the power to produce wealth. I pray I will never lack and always have more than enough. Bless me in all ways, including my finances. The more I make, the more I will give back to You. In Jesus' name, I pray. Amen.

## DAY 20

### I am filled with the Holy Spirit.
### I operate in all the fruit of the Spirit.

*And they were all filled with the Holy Spirit and began to speak with other tongues, as the Spirit gave them utterance.*
Acts 2:4 NKJV

*But the Holy Spirit produces this kind of fruit in our lives: love, joy, peace, patience, kindness, goodness, faithfulness, gentleness, and self-control. There is no law against these things!*
Galatians 5:22-23

If you have yet to receive the baptism of the Holy Spirit with the evidence of speaking in tongues, pray and ask God for it. It's available to you and me. It's not for just a select few.

> *For if you have the ability to speak in tongues, you will be talking only to God, since people won't be able to understand you. You will be speaking by the power of the Spirit, but it will all be mysterious.*
> 1 Corinthians 14:2

We began speaking in tongues when we were filled with the Holy Spirit. We need to continue to pray in the Spirit, even if we have only a few syllables/sounds. Ephesians 6:18 tells us to pray in the Spirit at all times and on every occasion. When we pray in the Spirit, we are talking to God.

If you've never been baptized in the Spirit with the evidence of speaking in tongues, pray this: God, I pray that You would baptize me now, Lord, with the Holy Spirit and fire. I know that it is for me, so I receive it now. Confirm that I have received with a heavenly prayer language in Jesus' name. Amen.

> *But when the Father sends the Advocate as my representative—that is, the Holy Spirit—he will teach you everything and will remind you of everything I have told you.*
> John 14:26

Jesus told His disciples the Holy Spirit would teach them everything and remind them of things He told them. It is very important that we are filled with the Spirit.

It is also imperative to ask the Lord to help us grow the fruit of the Spirit, which is different from being filled with the Holy Spirit.

FRUIT: A product of plant growth.[1]

The Holy Spirit produces fruit in us, which needs to be evident in our lives. If fruit is a product of plant growth, look at it this way. We are to be rooted in Christ. We get rooted in Him by reading the Word, and getting it into our Spirit. As our roots grow deeper, we develop and produce fruit.

We can walk in love, be joyful, have peace, be patient, show kindness, be good and faithful, be gentle and have self-control. These are the fruits of the Spirit. The more of these we exhibit, the more we grow into the person God wants us to be and become more like Jesus.

> *By their fruit you will recognize them. Do people pick grapes from thornbushes, or figs from thistles? Likewise, every good tree bears good fruit, but a bad tree bears bad fruit. A good tree cannot bear bad fruit, and a bad tree cannot bear good fruit.*
> Matthew 7:16-18 NIV

Just like you can tell what kind of tree a tree is by the fruit it bears, we can tell if a person is a follower of Christ by seeing the fruit of the Spirit in them.

## PRAYER

Father, I pray for a fresh filling of the Holy Spirit. Expand my heavenly prayer language. I want to be filled and overflowing with Your Spirit in me. I am also asking You to help me continue to develop the fruit of the Spirit. I want people to know I am a Christ follower by my fruit. Let people that don't know You see something different in me, something they want. Help me to always walk in love, be joyful, have peace, be patient, show kindness, be good and faithful, be gentle and have self-control. I know I can do this because I can do all things through Christ who strengthens me. I pray this in Jesus' name. Amen.

## DAY 21

> I declare that I am cared for.
> I will not be anxious about anything.

*Give all your worries and cares to God, for he cares about you.*
1 Peter 5:7

*Do not be anxious about anything, but in every situation, by prayer and petition, with thanksgiving, present your requests to God.*
Philippians 4:6 NIV

God cares about us. Let me say that again. God cares about you and me. He wants us to give Him our cares. He doesn't want us to be anxious about anything. This is easier said than done, but it's not impossible. We can go to God in prayer for every situation; it doesn't matter how big or small it is. We can do this. God cares about everything that concerns us. When we go to God, we can present our requests to Him, but we need to be sure to do so with thanksgiving.

At the time of writing this, I've been a mother for a little over 4 years. I care about every little thing concerning my son, and I mean every little thing. If I feel that way towards him and I am human, I can't imagine how much God loves us and cares about all that concerns us.

> *Give your burdens to the Lord, and he will take care of you. He will not permit the godly to slip and fall.*
> *Psalm 55:22*

God's got us. He's holding us and protecting us. We need to remain in His Word and obey what He wants us to do.

> *Come to me, all of you who are weary and carry heavy burdens, and I will give you rest. Take my yoke upon you. Let me teach you, because I am humble and gentle at heart, and you will find rest for your souls. For my yoke is easy to bear, and the burden I give you is light.*
> *Matthew 11:28-30*

Those are the words of Jesus, so let us cast our cares and heavy burdens on Him. He will exchange them for His light and easy burden.

ANXIOUS: Afraid or nervous especially about what may happen.[1]

God doesn't want us to be anxious. He doesn't want us to be afraid or nervous about what might happen. I dealt with anxiety and lots of physical symptoms of it for years. But I knew God's Word, so I kept repeating His promises over and over and I gained the victory.

There still may be times when these feelings of anxiousness try to creep back in, but once I realize it, I do my best to cast those cares on God and remind myself I don't need to be anxious. We must trust that God is who He says He is and will do what He promises.

## PRAYER

Father, I thank You that I can cast my cares on You, for You care for me. You don't want me to be anxious. So I come to You in prayer and I present my requests to You. I thank You that You are who You say You are and will do what You have promised. You are faithful. When situations make me feel anxious, may Your Words flood my heart and mind, and the anxiety will flee. I know I can trust in You. Jesus tells me to give Him my heavy burden, and He will give me rest, so I lay my burdens at Your feet. I pray this in Jesus' name. Amen.

## DAY 22

**I declare that I am redeemed.
I have the blessing of Abraham.**

*Christ has redeemed us from the curse of the law, having become a curse for us (for it is written, "Cursed is everyone who hangs on a tree"), that the blessing of Abraham might come upon the Gentiles in Christ Jesus, that we might receive the promise of the Spirit through faith.*

*Galatians 3:13-14 NKJV*

Christ has redeemed us from the curse of the law. Can I get a shout of praise!? If you don't know what the curse of the law is, you can read it in Deuteronomy 28. It's a terrible curse! Part of that curse is sickness and poverty. Praise be to Jesus Christ for redeeming us!

When Jesus died on the cross, He did it for us. He took our place so that the curse would no longer be able to come on us. Not only that, but now we have access to the blessing of Abraham because of what Christ did for us.

> REDEEM: To buy back. To free from a lien by payment of an amount secured thereby.[1]

Jesus redeemed us. He paid the price for us in full. When something is paid for in full, it doesn't need to be paid for again. It's a done deal. If I go to the grocery store with my son and I pay for my groceries, nobody goes up to my son afterwards asking him to pay for them too. He would say, "My mom already bought them, so I don't have to."

We need this to become a known fact in our minds and hearts. We are redeemed! Jesus redeemed us. What did he redeem us from? The curse of the law includes sickness, poverty, lack, etc. We are healed and whole.

What is the blessing of Abraham?

> *I will make you into a great nation, and I will bless you; I will make your name great, and you will be a blessing. I will bless those who bless you, and whoever curses you I will curse; and all peoples on earth will be blessed through you.*
> *Genesis 12:2-3 NKJV*

In Genesis 17:1-8 God establishes a covenant with Abraham.

> *I will establish my covenant as an everlasting covenant between me and you and your descendants after you for the generations to come, to be your God and the God of your descendants after you.*
>
> Genesis 17:7 NIV

God blessed Abraham, God prospered Abraham, and God took care of Abraham. Abraham lived a long, good, healthy life.

> *And now that you belong to Christ, you are the true children of Abraham. You are his heirs, and God's promise to Abraham belongs to you.*
>
> Galatians 3:29

God's promises to Abraham belong to us. Thank You, Lord!

## PRAYER

Father, thank You that I am redeemed from the curse of the law because Christ has redeemed me. I no longer need to deal with the curse of the law in my life. I will speak to my situations and tell them to align with Your Word. I know I am redeemed. Jesus paid the price in full. It's Your will for me to be healed, healthy, and whole. It is Your will for me to be prosperous and full of joy and peace. I thank You that the blessing of Abraham belongs to me. In Jesus' name, I pray. Amen.

## DAY 23

> I declare that I am transformed.
> I live in God's good and pleasing
> and perfect will for my life.

*Don't copy the behavior and customs of this world, but let God transform you into a new person by changing the way you think. Then you will learn to know God's will for you, which is good and pleasing and perfect.*
*Romans 12:2*

How can we let God transform the way we think? You can probably guess. I've said it multiple times already because it's the truth and so important. We need to get into His Word.

> *So then faith comes by hearing, and hearing by the word of God.*
> *Romans 10:17 NKJV*

As we learn more about God and meditate on His Word, it changes us from the inside. We will not want to do things God disapproves of in this world.

I changed a lot during my first years as a Christian. The first thing I felt the Spirit leading me to do was to stop drinking alcohol, then stop going to clubs and bars, then start dressing modestly, etc. The Spirit led me to change the music I listened to, the shows I watched, etc.

The Spirit is still leading me to make changes when necessary. We never get to the point where we no longer need to be transformed. The process is making us more like Jesus. We need to continue to let God transform us from the inside out.

When we are set on living according to God's Word, we will know God's good and pleasing and perfect will for our lives. That's where we should all want to be.

I know I want that, do you? To be transformed, don't copy the behaviours and customs of this world. If we live like everyone else, like non-Christians, then we are not being transformed. We need to be different. That's how people will know that we are God's children.

> TRANSFORM: To change in composition or structure. To change in character or condition.[1]

We need to let God continue to transform us, change our character, and make us more like Jesus every day.

*...and the Lord—who is the Spirit—makes us more and more like him as we are changed into his glorious image."*
*2 Corinthians 3:18*

We need to allow Him to change us; He won't force us to change. God has given us free will. We get to make the choice. Choosing not to be transformed is still a choice.

*So you must live as God's obedient children. Don't slip back into your old ways of living to satisfy your own desires. You didn't know any better then. But now you must be holy in everything you do, just as God who chose you is holy. For the Scriptures say, "You must be holy because I am holy."*
*1 Peter 1:14-16*

God is not asking us to give things up or giving us a list of rules to make life boring. Being transformed is for our benefit. The thief's purpose is to steal, kill, and destroy. But Jesus' purpose is to give us a rich and satisfying life. (John 10:10) God is good, loves us so much, and wants the best for us, but we need to be willing to make the changes He asks us to make.

## PRAYER

Father, thank You that I don't need to copy the behaviours and customs of this world, though sometimes, they seem enjoyable. Help me to not want to be like everyone else. I want to be different. I want to be transformed and be who You've called me to be. Transform me into the person You want me to be. I want to know Your good and perfect and pleasing will for my life. Make me more like Jesus. In Jesus' name, I pray. Amen.

# DAY 24

I declare that I have peace at all times and in all situations.
I have perfect peace.
I have peace in my mind and heart.

*Now may the Lord of peace himself give you his peace at all times and in every situation. The Lord be with you all.*
*2 Thessalonians 3:16*

*You will keep in perfect peace all who trust in you, all whose thoughts are fixed on you!*
*Isaiah 26:3*

*"I am leaving you with a gift-peace of mind and heart. And the peace I give is a gift the world cannot give. So don't be troubled or afraid.*
*John 14:7*

PERFECT: Being entirely without fault or defect.[1]

God's will for us is to stay in perfect peace as we trust Him. That means that peace is entirely without fault or defect. He gives us His perfect peace. He wants us to be at peace at all times and in every situation. It is strange to think that's possible, but God wants it to be our reality.

God's peace is not the peace the world gives.

> *And the peace of God, which surpasses all understanding, will guard your hearts and minds through Christ Jesus.*
> *Philippians 4:7 NKJV*

> *For God is not the author of confusion but of peace...*
> *1 Corinthians 14:33 NKJV*

If you are confused, know that it doesn't come from God. Get into His Word, pray, and ask Him to speak to you to give you clarity and peace. If you need wisdom, ask, and He will give it to you. God wants us to have peace in our hearts and minds; it's a gift from Him. Will you receive it?

You may be wondering how it's possible, given your circumstances. I don't know what you are going through, but I know God's Word is true.

> *For just as the heavens are higher than the earth, so my ways are higher than your ways and my thoughts higher than your thoughts.*
> *Isaiah 55:9*

We need to trust God. We need to stay rooted in Him and His Word, trusting Him, knowing He is a good God and works all things for good for those who love Him and are called according to His purpose (Romans 8:28).

May our thoughts be fixed on God and His Word. He doesn't want us to be afraid or troubled. Let us do our best to receive this peace He wants us to have.

> *Now may the Lord of peace himself give you his peace at all times and in every situation. The Lord be with you all.*
> *2 Thessalonians 3:16*

His peace. At all times. In every situation. Yes, please!

## PRAYER

Father, I thank You that You keep me in perfect peace as I trust in You. Thank You that You want me to live in peace at all times and in every situation. I thank You that You give perfect peace. You don't want me to be troubled or afraid. When I don't feel at peace, I pray Your Word will flood my thoughts and remind me to keep my peace. I trust You, Lord. I pray that all things will work together for my good because I love You and I am called according to Your purpose. You are good. In Jesus' name, I pray. Amen.

## DAY 25

### I declare that I am gifted. I am qualified.

*In his grace, God has given us different gifts for doing certain things well. So if God has given you the ability to prophesy, speak out with as much faith as God has given you. If your gift is serving others, serve them well. If you are a teacher, teach well. If your gift is to encourage others, be encouraging. If it is giving, give generously. If God has given you leadership ability, take the responsibility seriously. And if you have a gift for showing kindness to others, do it gladly.*
*Romans 12:6-8*

*It is not that we think we are qualified to do anything on our own. Our qualification comes from God.*
*2 Corinthians 3:5*

We all have unique gifts that God has chosen to give each of us. What are your gifts? Are you using your gifts to bring glory to God? If you don't know what your gifts are, pray and ask God.

God is not looking at our past and wanting to condemn us. He's not looking at our weaknesses and judging us for them. God is not like humans. When God looks at us, He sees our potential and all we can be.

> QUALIFIED: Fitted (as by training or experience) for a given purpose.[1]

God has a given purpose for each of us. God doesn't make mistakes. You are here for a reason. You were born for such a time as this (Esther 4:14).

> ... He has created us anew in Christ Jesus, so we can do the good things he planned for us long ago.
> *Ephesians 2:10*

What are you good at? What makes you happy? What are your gifts? The answers to the first two questions give you an indication of what your giftings are.

God equips us to do what He wants us to do. He wants what we do to be enjoyable. Take time to pray and ask God in what areas He has gifted you and how to use those gifts to bring Him glory.

> *Work willingly at whatever you do, as though you were working for the Lord rather than for people.*
> *Colossians 3:23*

> *And whatever you do or say, do it as a representative of the Lord Jesus, giving thanks through him to God the Father.*
> *Colossians 3:17*

*So whether you eat or drink, or whatever you do, do it all for the glory of God.*
                              *1 Corinthians 10:31*

Whatever we do, it should all be done for the glory of God. So even if you don't know what your "gifts" are, all you do should still glorify our Lord and Saviour.

## PRAYER

Father, thank You that You have gifted me. Help me to know how You gifted me and to be confident in the gifts You've given me. Teach me to use my gifts in a way that brings You glory. I'm so glad my qualification comes from You. I want all that I do to bring You glory. In Jesus' name, I pray. Amen.

## DAY 26

### I declare that I am a mountain mover. I am confident God answers prayer.

*Then Jesus said to the disciples, "Have faith in God. I tell you the truth, you can say to this mountain, 'May you be lifted up and thrown into the sea,' and it will happen. But you must really believe it will happen and have no doubt in your heart."*

*Mark 11:22-23*

*And we are confident that he hears us whenever we ask for anything that pleases him. And since we know he hears us when we make our requests, we also know that he will give us what we ask for.*

*1 John 5:14-15*

God is good. God is faithful. His Word tells us that we can ask for anything (as long as it's in line with His will, which is His Word), and it will be done for us. We are to not doubt. We are to believe. God is who He says He is and will do what He has promised. We need to remove all doubt.

"Don't doubt your faith; doubt your doubts, for they are unreliable."[1] (F.F. Bosworth, Christ the Healer)

We need to trust God, and He will show Himself faithful. Don't doubt God. Doubt your doubts.

How do we remove doubt? We need to fill ourselves with the truth of God's Word. What are you praying for? Find scriptures that support it. This is so important to do.

Here are a couple of examples to help get you started.

Healing - Isaiah 53:4-5, Psalm 103:2-3, 1 Peter 2:24

Provision - Jeremiah 29:11, Psalm 1:1-3, 2 Corinthians 8:9

CONFIDENT: Full of conviction, certain.[2]

We need to be certain that God will answer prayers that align with His Word.

> *It is the same with my word. I send it out, and it always produces fruit. It will accomplish all I want it to, and it will prosper everywhere I send it.*
> *Isaiah 55:11*

God's Word will not return to Him void. If God told us in His Word that He would do something, we can stand on that promise, and He will make it happen. Mountains will move.

We are to pray to the Father in Jesus' name. Use scripture. We need to find scriptures that align with what we're asking for when we pray. Know that God will answer.

*At that time you won't need to ask me for anything. I tell you the truth, you will ask the Father directly, and he will grant your request because you use my name. You haven't done this before. Ask, using my name, and you will receive, and you will have abundant joy.*
John 16:23-24

*You can ask for anything in my name, and I will do it, so that the Son can bring glory to the Father. Yes, ask me for anything in my name, and I will do it!*
John 14:13-14

Jesus said that! When you pray, pray to the Father in Jesus' name and use scripture to support your request. Then be confident that God will answer.

## PRAYER

Father, thank You that You hear me when I pray and that You are a prayer answering God. Help me remove all doubt. I will not doubt You; I will doubt my doubts. You are able to do what You say in Your Word You will do. Your Word will not return to You void. It will accomplish its purpose. I have faith in You. I am a mountain mover. No mountain can stand in my way. I trust You. I'm confident in You. In Jesus' name, I pray. Amen.

## DAY 27

**I declare that I am guarding my heart. I trust in the Lord.**

*Guard your heart above all else, for it determines the course of your life.*
*Proverbs 4:23*

*Trust in the Lord with all your heart; do not depend on your own understanding.*
*Proverbs 3:5*

We must guard our hearts. How do we do that? We must be careful what we let into us, what we watch, and what we listen to. It all affects us. We can't be listening to music about infidelity and watching movies about infidelity all the time and keeping our hearts pure and on course with what God wants.

I won't tell you what you can and can't watch. There's no "list" like that. But I will say if you feel conviction, stop it, whatever it is, whether it be a movie or show you are watching or a song or music you're listening to. Also, if you notice it influences you, not in a good way, stop it.

I've been a Christian for over a decade, and there are movies I watched a few years ago that now, I feel convicted if I want to watch them, so I don't. Even if other Christians don't understand because they don't have the same conviction, I won't ignore my convictions.

When we do our part, God does His. We can trust in Him. He will direct us. We need to listen to His instruction. Let us be sensitive to what God is speaking to us to do or not do.

> *A good person produces good things from the treasury of a good heart, and an evil person produces evil things from the treasury of an evil heart. What you say flows from what is in your heart.*
>
> *Luke 6:45*

What is in your heart will come out. It's a hard truth. Many people have used the expression, "Oops, sorry, I didn't mean to say that," but in all seriousness, it had to have come from somewhere. Where? Your heart. What's in your heart?

GUARD: A defensive state or attitude.[1]

We need to guard our hearts, and it's not something to take lightly. Just because everyone you know is watching a particular movie, and they are Christians too, doesn't mean you have to if you have a conviction from the Spirit. Not that it's wrong, but is it right? Can you still watch it? Sure. Will you go to hell if you do? Probably not. But should you watch it? You decide.

> *Avoid all perverse talk; stay away from corrupt speech. Look straight ahead, and fix your eyes on what lies before you. Mark out a straight path for your feet; stay on the safe path. Don't get sidetracked; keep your feet from following evil.*
> *Proverbs 4:24-27*

Let us guard our hearts. Let us be careful what comes out of our mouths and not get sidetracked. Listen to the Holy Spirit; He will guide us.

God knows everything. Even if you can hide your secrets from everyone else, you can't hide from God.

## PRAYER

Father, I want to guard my heart carefully. Help me and speak to me about what I need to do and not do to be better at guarding my heart. I trust You, even when I don't understand all that's going on. I will not depend on my own understanding but continue to trust in You knowing that You work all things out for my good. I want my heart to be healthy and pure. Burn out all the things in me that are not from You. Help me guard my eyes and ears, watch what I say, what I do with my hands and feet, and what I let into my heart and mind. In Jesus' name, I pray. Amen.

## DAY 28

> I declare that I am hopeful about my future.
> I know God works all things together for my good.
> I am created for a purpose.

*"For I know the plans I have for you," declares the Lord, "plans to prosper you and not to harm you, plans to give you hope and a future."*
Jeremiah 29:11 NIV

*And we know that God causes everything to work together for the good of those who love God and are called according to his purpose for them.*
Romans 8:28

God has good plans for us, to give us a future and a hope. Not only that, but God works all things together for our good. The enemy may try and attack, but God will give us victory every time. We need to know that God is good. If something is not good, it does not come from God. God can turn things that are not good for us around and use them for His glory. Every good and perfect gift comes from God (James 1:17), so if it's not good, it's not from God.

> *You parents—if your children ask for a loaf of bread, do you give them a stone instead? Or if they ask for a fish, do you give them a snake? Of course not! So if you sinful people know how to give good gifts to your children, how much more will your heavenly Father give good gifts to those who ask him.*
> *Matthew 7:9-11*

> *And you know that God anointed Jesus of Nazareth with the Holy Spirit and with power. Then Jesus went around doing good and healing all who were oppressed by the devil, for God was with him.*
> *Acts 10:38*

> *The thief does not come except to steal, and to kill, and to destroy. I have come that they may have life, and that they may have it more abundantly.*
> *John 10:10 NKJV*

If it steals, kills or destroys, it's from the enemy. If it's life-giving and good, it comes from God. God = good. Devil = bad. It's pretty simple when we think about it like that. If things are happening in your life that are not good, they are sent by satan. Don't blame God. Pray to God, ask Him why, repent of sin, ask God how to get out of it, and remind Him of His Word.

God can turn all things, even bad things, for good, for those who love Him, but He's never the one who sends the bad thing in the first place.

> HOPE: Desire accompanied by expectation of or belief in fulfillment.[1]

God gives us hope. We can expect good things to happen to us. I have a sign that says, "Always believe something good is going to happen," hanging on a wall in my room. We should live with the expectation that good things will happen to us and through us every day.

## PRAYER

Father, I thank You that You have plans to prosper me and to give me hope and a future. Thank You that You work all things for good in my life. I know that if something is not good, it is not from You. You know the things that are not good in my life. I pray You help me to understand why and what I can do so You can turn it around for my good. Forgive me of sins I've committed. I trust You to work things out for me. I pray that something good will happen to me today. I expect to see Your goodness in my life every day. In Jesus' name, I pray. Amen.

## DAY 29

> I declare that I am fearfully
> and wonderfully made.
> I am beautiful.

*I praise you because I am fearfully and wonderfully made; your works are wonderful, I know that full well.*
                              Psalm 139:14 NIV

God knit us together in our mother's wombs. We are all unique, all important, and all special in the way God made us. He knows every detail of our bodies and our lives. No one thinks about us as much as God does. No one cares about us as much as God does. No one loves us as much as God does. We are all beautiful because God made us. We need to love ourselves as God made us.

> WONDERFULLY: In a way or to an extent that excites wonder, astonishment, or amazement.[1]

We are wonderfully made. Do not let anyone tell you or make you feel otherwise. I know it's easier said than done, but let us be confident in who we are and who God created us to be.

Beauty is in the eye of the beholder. It's a relative term. God's not looking at your race, weight, age, skin colour or anything like that. God looks at the heart. That's where true beauty is found.

> *But the Lord said to Samuel, "Don't judge by his appearance or height, for I have rejected him. The Lord doesn't see things the way you see them. People judge by outward appearance, but the Lord looks at the heart."*
> *1 Samuel 16:7*

If your heart is beautiful, then you are beautiful indeed. That's what really matters, and that's what matters most to God.

> *Charm is deceptive, and beauty does not last; but a woman who fears the Lord will be greatly praised.*
> *Proverbs 31:30*

Outward "beauty" doesn't last. We live in a day and age where social media and filters set such high expectations for women and what they "should" look like to be considered beautiful.

It doesn't help that so many people have started offering different types of procedures to alter the body; breast augmentation, liposuction, lash lift, lash tint, lash extensions, hair extensions, eyebrow fillers, makeup tattooing, tanning salons and tanning sprays, etc. It's not just lipstick and mascara; now it's our entire image that the world is trying to "change" so we can look "more" beautiful. To who? Let your beauty be more than just on the outside to impress the people around you.

Let's be beautiful from the inside out.

## PRAYER

Father, thank You that You made me in my mother's womb. You chose me to be who I am, and I am thankful. I will not compare myself to the world's beauty standards, but help me search the Bible for Your definition of beauty, and I will do my best to be beautiful from the inside out. In Jesus' name, I pray. Amen.

## DAY 30

### I declare that I will praise the Lord with my whole heart.

*Let all that I am praise the Lord; with my whole heart, I will praise his holy name. Let all that I am praise the Lord; may I never forget the good things he does for me. He forgives all my sins and heals all my diseases. He redeems me from death and crowns me with love and tender mercies. He fills my life with good things. My youth is renewed like the eagle's!*

*Psalm 103:1-5*

We need to ensure we never forget the good things God does for us.

1. He forgives all our sins.
2. He heals our diseases.
3. He redeems us from death and destruction.
4. He crowns us with love and tender mercies.
5. He fills our lives with good things.
6. Our youth is renewed like the eagles.

Look at all God has provided for us. We must praise the Lord with all we are. God is so good!

> RENEW: To make like new, restore to freshness, vigor, or perfection.[1]

If you're in your 20's, that last one might not matter so much, but when you get to your 40's or 50's or 60's and upwards, or if you're there now, that's a pretty great thing to remember. We don't need to be frail as we get older. God will renew our youth.

> *But those who hope in the Lord will renew their strength. They will soar on wings like eagles; they will run and not grow weary, they will walk and not be faint.*
> *Isaiah 40:31 NIV*

Let us hope in the Lord and praise Him. He will renew our strength. We will not grow weary or faint.

We need to trust God, obey God, love God and give Him praise. He is good. We need to get into the Word, let it become real to us and fill our hearts and minds with His truth. When we know all He's done for us, we can't help but praise the Lord with all our hearts.

*Praise the Lord! Praise God in his sanctuary; praise him in his mighty heaven! Praise him for his mighty works; praise his unequaled greatness! Praise him with a blast of the ram's horn; praise him with the lyre and harp! Praise him with the tambourine and dancing; praise him with strings and flutes! Praise him with a clash of cymbals; praise him with loud clanging cymbals. Let everything that breathes sing praises to the Lord! Praise the Lord!*

*Psalm 150:1-6*

Let us praise the Lord with all our hearts, at all times, with all that is within us.

## PRAYER

Father, thank You for all You do for me; may I never forget it. I will praise You, Lord, with my whole heart. Thank You that You forgive all my sins. Thank You that You heal all my diseases. Thank You that You've redeemed me from death and destruction. Thank You that You cover me with love and tender mercies. Thank You that You fill my life with good things. Thank You that You renew my youth like the eagles. I pray all this in Jesus' name. Amen.

# DAY 31

**I declare that I am a woman with worth.
I am valuable.
I am God's masterpiece.**

*Look at the ravens. They don't plant or harvest or store food in barns, for God feeds them. And you are far more valuable to him than any birds!*
*Luke 12:24*

*For we are God's masterpiece. He has created us anew in Christ Jesus, so we can do the good things he planned for us long ago.*
*Ephesians 2:10*

There's no one like you, no not one. There's only one you! Even identical twins are not exactly the same. We are all unique. God cares for us more than we know. We are so valuable to Him. We are His masterpieces. We have worth because God made us.

> MASTERPIECE: A work done with extraordinary skill.[1]

God made each of us a masterpiece. He made us who we are with extraordinary skill.

> ... you are more valuable to God than a whole flock of sparrows.
> Matthew 10:31

> How precious are your thoughts about me, O God. They cannot be numbered! I can't even count them; they outnumber the grains of sand! And when I wake up, you are still with me!
> Psalm 139:17-18

God's thoughts about us outnumber the grains of sand. He knew us before we were born. His love for us is more significant than we can comprehend.

When I became a mother, the love I felt and still feel for my son is a love I had never felt before. There is something truly special about a mother's love for her child. To imagine that God loves my son more than me is beyond me, but I know He does. God's love for each of us is greater than any love we will experience from anyone else. This is why we can rest assured that we are valuable to God.

> For you created my inmost being; you knit me together in my mother's womb. I praise you because I am fearfully and wonderfully made; your works are wonderful, I know that full well.
> Psalm 139:13-14 NIV

God doesn't make mistakes. Let us praise God for who we are.

You, yes YOU, reading this right now. You are a woman with worth! Keep your head held high. Know you are who God says you are no matter what others say. If you love God and obey Him and keep His Word, nothing and no one can stop you from doing what God has called you to do.

You have a purpose. You are here for a reason. Trust God. He is good. He loves you. He wants the best for you. Don't ever forget it.

## PRAYER

Father, thank You for making me who I am. There is only one of me! You made me, and You called me and chose me. I love You! I want You to speak to me as I read Your Word. I will do my best to do my part, and You will do Your part and keep Your promises to me. Thank You that I am a woman with worth. I will praise You every day. In Jesus' name, I pray. Amen.

If you have a testimony on how this devotional has encouraged you, please email me at joeanne@joeannechamberlain.com.

I'd love to hear from you!

## ABOUT ME - THE AUTHOR

I was born and raised in Toronto, Ontario. I accepted Jesus as my Lord and Saviour when I was 23. I got married in 2017 to my husband, Nick. In 2019, I had my son, Joseph, who is a gift from God. I love my family of three.

I'm a WFHM (work-from-home-mom), and I am home-schooling my son. I love writing, designing, event planning and playing board games. My husband currently works full-time for the church we attend. Our small business (Chamberlain Creative) does graphic design, print, video, photo and vinyl. We also love playing family-friendly board games and are creating some of our own (Enjay Games).

I love to encourage other women, especially new moms. I enjoy reading the Bible, listening to podcasts and watching some of my favourites live on YouTube or their apps. I enjoy reading books written by men and women that God used/uses to do noteable works, the works that Jesus did.

Here are a few of my favourites in alphabetical order:
- Jonathan & Adalis Shuttlesworth (Revival Today Church)
- Kenneth & Gloria Copeland (Kenneth Copeland Ministries)
- Nathan & MaryAnn Pimentel (Household of Faith Ministries)
- Smith Wigglesworth
- Ted & Carolyn Shuttlesworth (Miracle Word Ministries)
- Ted Shuttlesworth Sr. (Faith Alive)
- Tiff & Judy Shuttlesworth (Lost Lamb Association)
- TJ & Kerry Malcangi (Salvation Now)
- TL Osborn

Follow me on Instagram, Facebook and TikTok
@joeannechamberlain

# SOME OF MY FAVOURITE BOOKS

The Holy Bible

Healing The Sick by TL Osborn

Dominion Over Sickness & Disease by Jonathan Shuttlesworth

Blood on the Door by Ted Shuttlesworth Jr.

Praise. Laugh. Repeat. by Ted Shuttlesworth Jr.

The Believers Authority by Kenneth E. Haggin

Unhang Your Harp by Ted Shuttlesworth Jr.

Limitless Love by Kenneth & Gloria Copeland

Financial Overflow by Jonathan Shuttlesworth

20 Secrets to an Unbreakable Marriage by Jonathan & Adalis Shuttlesworth

Raising Children with a Passion to Know and Serve Jesus Christ by Judy Shuttlesworth

These are a few of the books I consider MUST READS.

# ACKNOWLEDGEMENTS

**God**, thank You for saving me, loving me and trusting me to write this book. I thank You that You are who You say You are, and You will do what You have promised. Your Word will not return to You void; You keep Your promises. To You be all the glory. I love You, Lord.

**Nick**, thank you for your love and support and your encouragement to take the time to work on this book. Thank you for teaching me the programs I wanted to write my book in and for helping me design my cover. I'm so glad God brought you into my life. I love you, babe.

**Joseph**, thank you for the best cuddles as I worked on parts of this book during your quiet time. You are my sweet boy, and you bring me so much joy. I'm so glad God picked me to be your Mama. You will always be my baby boy, no matter how old you are. I love you, sweetheart.

In alphabetical order -**Judy, Kerry, Leanna & MaryAnn**- thank you, ladies, for taking the time to read my manuscript and give me your feedback. I have great respect for you all. You were the first four women to read this devotional, and I genuinely appreciate it.

**You**, reading this book, thank you! I pray this book is a blessing to you and that as you keep reading through it, God's Word and these biblical declarations will help you grow stronger in your faith and deeper in your relationship with God. The best is yet to come!

# NOTES

**Introduction (*on the back cover as well)**
[1] "declare." *Britannica.com/dictionary*. Britannica, 2023. March 5, 2023.

**Day 1**
[1] "saved." *Merriam-Webster.com*. Merriam-Webster, 2023. March 5, 2023.

**Day 2**
[1] "adopted." *Merriam-Webster.com*. Merriam-Webster, 2023. March 5, 2023.

**Day 3**
[1] "whoever." *Merriam-Webster.com*. Merriam-Webster, 2023. March 5, 2023.

**Day 4**
[1] "sin." *Britannica.com/dictionary*. Britannica, 2023. March 5, 2023.

**Day 5**
[1] "chosen." *Merriam-Webster.com*. Merriam-Webster, 2023. March 5, 2023.

**Day 6**
[1] "strength." *Merriam-Webster.com*. Merriam-Webster, 2023. March 5, 2023.

**Day 7**
[1] "heal." *Merriam-Webster.com*. Merriam-Webster, 2023. March 5, 2023.

**Day 8**
[1] "overflow." *Merriam-Webster.com*. Merriam-Webster, 2023. March 5, 2023.

[2] Cooke, George W. Lyrics to "Down in My Heart." Performed by Cedarmont Kids, 1995. *Lyrics.com*, https://www.lyrics.com/lyric/1488236/Cedarmont+Kids/Down+in+My+Heart

**Day 9**
[1] "protect." *Merriam-Webster.com*. Merriam-Webster, 2023. March 5, 2023.

**Day 10**
[1] "secure." *Merriam-Webster.com. Merriam-Webster,* 2023. March 5, 2023.

**Day 11**
[1] "mediate." *Merriam-Webster.com. Merriam-Webster,* 2023. March 5, 2023.

**Day 12**
[1] "armor." *Merriam-Webster.com. Merriam-Webster,* 2023. March 5, 2023.

**Day 13**
[1] "wisdom." *Britannica.com/dictionary. Britannica,* 2023. March 5, 2023.

**Day 14**
[1] "authority." *Britannica.com/dictionary. Britannica,* 2023. March 5, 2023.

**Day 15**
[1] "victory." *Britannica.com/dictionary. Britannica,* 2023. March 5, 2023.

**Day 16**
[1] "fear." *Merriam-Webster.com. Merriam-Webster,* 2023. March 5, 2023.

**Day 17**
[1] "root." *Britannica.com/dictionary. Britannica,* 2023. March 5, 2023.

**Day 18**
[1] "firm." *Merriam-Webster.com. Merriam-Webster,* 2023. March 5, 2023.

**Day 19**
[1] "rich." *Merriam-Webster.com. Merriam-Webster,* 2023. March 5, 2023.

**Day 20**
[1] "fruit." *Merriam-Webster.com. Merriam-Webster,* 2023. March 5, 2023.

**Day 21**
[1] "anxious." *Britannica.com/dictionary. Britannica,* 2023. March 5, 2023.

**Day 22**
[1] "redeem." *Merriam-Webster.com. Merriam-Webster,* 2023.
March 5, 2023.

**Day 23**
[1] "transform." *Merriam-Webster.com. Merriam-Webster,* 2023.
March 5, 2023.

**Day 24**
[1] "perfect." *Merriam-Webster.com. Merriam-Webster,* 2023.
March 5, 2023.

**Day 25**
[1] "qualified." *Merriam-Webster.com. Merriam-Webster,* 2023.
March 5, 2023.

**Day 26**
[1] Bosworth, F.F. (2008). Christ The Healer. Chosen Books.

[2] "confident." *Merriam-Webster.com. Merriam-Webster,* 2023.
March 5, 2023.

**Day 27**
[1] "guard." *Merriam-Webster.com. Merriam-Webster,* 2023.
March 5, 2023.

**Day 28**
[1] "hope." *Merriam-Webster.com. Merriam-Webster,* 2023.
March 5, 2023.

**Day 29**
[1] "wonderfully." *Merriam-Webster.com. Merriam-Webster,* 2023.
March 5, 2023.

**Day 30**
[1] "renew." *Merriam-Webster.com. Merriam-Webster,* 2023.
March 5, 2023.

**Day 31**
[1] "masterpiece." *Merriam-Webster.com. Merriam-Webster,* 2023.
March 5, 2023.

Manufactured by Amazon.ca
Bolton, ON

34569126R00063